Praise for The Clear Light

"From the opening poem, a loving invitation to meet in the purity of presence, to the closing parable of the wave that falls in love with itself and forgets it's the ocean, Steve Taylor has gifted us with a collection of illuminating, heartful incantations, meditations, reflections, and above all, direct pointers to our non-dual spiritual nature, in which all our unhealed suffering and trauma resolve in the 'clear light of the present.' This is a book to dip into and savor again and again."

— **Stephan Bodian**, author of
Wake Up Now and *Beyond Mindfulness*

"Each poem in this book offers us a beautiful piece of wisdom. Steve Taylor writes with the quiet, humble assurance of a Zen master and also with sparks of the passion of Rumi and Hafiz. This book is an absolute must-read for anyone on a spiritual path in need of guidance on how best to live their daily life with mindfulness, heart, and equanimity. The gift of *The Clear Light* is that it gently wakes us up. I guarantee that if you spend a few days simply allowing Steve's words to percolate into your heart, you will find that your consciousness expands."

— **Serge Beddington-Behrens**, author of
Awakening the Universal Heart and *Gateways to the Soul*

"In this time of anxiety about the future, Steve Taylor brings us the gift of poetic meditations to rest deeply in the living, loving now. He invites us not just to rest but also to be openly compassionate and to live courageously. Keep *The Clear Light* close by to nourish your spirit."

— **Loch Kelly**, author of
The Way of Effortless Mindfulness

THE Clear Light

Also by Steve Taylor

Out of Time

The Fall

Making Time

Waking from Sleep

Out of the Darkness

Back to Sanity

The Meaning

Not I, Not Other Than I:
The Life and Teachings of Russel Williams

The Calm Center

The Leap

Spiritual Science

THE Clear Light

Spiritual Reflections and Meditations

STEVE TAYLOR

Foreword by ECKHART TOLLE

• An Eckhart Tolle Edition •

New World Library
Novato, California

An Eckhart Tolle Edition
www.eckharttolle.com

New World Library
14 Pamaron Way
Novato, California 94949

Text design by Tona Pearce Myers

Library of Congress Cataloging-in-Publication Data

Names: Taylor, Steve, date, author.
Title: The clear light : spiritual reflections and meditations / Steve Taylor ; introduction by Eckhart Tolle.
Description: Novato, California : New World Library, [2020] | "An Eckhart Tolle edition" | Summary: "A collection of brief lyric poems about meditation, spiritual enlightenment, and the search for transcendence."-- Provided by publisher.
Identifiers: LCCN 2020025512 (print) | LCCN 2020025513 (ebook) | ISBN 9781608687121 (hardcover) | ISBN 9781608687138 (epub)
Subjects: LCGFT: Poetry.
Classification: LCC PR6120.A97 C57 2020 (print) | LCC PR6120.A97 (ebook) | DDC 821/.92--dc23
LC record available at https://lccn.loc.gov/2020025512
LC ebook record available at https://lccn.loc.gov/2020025513

First printing, September 2020
ISBN 978-1-60868-712-1
Ebook ISBN 978-1-60868-713-8
Printed in the United States on 30% postconsumer-waste recycled paper

New World Library is proud to be a Gold Certified Environmentally Responsible Publisher. Publisher certification awarded by Green Press Initiative.

10 9 8 7 6 5 4 3 2

Contents

Foreword

And God said, "Let there be light,"
and there was light.

According to Genesis, the first book of the Bible, the creation of light preceded even the creation of the sun and the other celestial bodies.

In fact, this light appears to be a prerequisite for the creation of the cosmos (a Greek word that translates as "order"). It is clearly the case, therefore, that the word *light* is used here to refer to something much deeper than that which can be perceived by our sense of sight. It is a word derived from the realm of sensory perception, but it points to a mystery that is prior to and beyond the world of appearances and manifestation. Perhaps we could describe it as the organizing principle that guides the evolution of life throughout the universe, an infinite, eternal, and transcendent consciousness that gradually expresses itself more and more fully in the dimension of space and time. This would imply that the creation of the universe is by no means finished yet, but is a process that is ongoing, and that humans, too, are a work in progress. There is an evolutionary impulse that drives all life-forms toward greater consciousness, toward enLIGHTenment!

When Jesus said, "You are the light of the world" (Matthew 5:14), he was speaking to every human being. He was able to make this assertion because he had realized this reality within himself and was therefore able to state unequivocally, "I am the light of the world" (John 8:12).

Similarly, in Mahayana Buddhism, the term *clear light* is synonymous with *luminous mind*, which refers to the Buddha-nature that is the essence deep within every life-form.

Steve Taylor's *The Clear Light* is not only a book of inspiring spiritual and poetic reflections, but also a powerful and invaluable guide to the realization of who or what you are beyond the conditioned mind. If you read this book slowly, attentively, and repeatedly, it can take you beyond identification with the content of your mind and into the clear light of present-moment awareness. This book will show you how every situation you encounter can become an opening into the state of presence. Performing a routine task is suddenly experienced as deeply fulfilling; you discover magic in ordinary, everyday objects; being present in nature gives you a glimpse of sacredness and self-transcendence; and even stress, conflict, and suffering can bring about a spiritual awakening.

If used rightly (and if you are ready), this book can transform your state of consciousness as you read. You then no longer derive your sense of identity from your personal history, but from a much deeper place, and you realize that you are, indeed, the light of the world.

— Eckhart Tolle, author of
The Power of Now and *A New Earth*

Meeting Purely in Presence

Let's meet without pretense
without hierarchies of status
or artificial shows of respect
without trying to impress each other
with our knowledge or charm or humor.

Let's meet without fear
of exposing our vulnerabilities
without being embarrassed by our need for love
or pretending to be self-sufficient.

Let's meet without the past
without letting our urge to connect
be obstructed by old resentments
without letting our natural empathy
be blocked by hard, fixed prejudice.

Let's meet without insecurity
knowing that we don't have to prove
that we're worthy of each other's affection
since love doesn't need to be earned or gained
but simply allowed to flow.

Let's meet without intentions
without any designs or goals
knowing we don't have to try to relate to each other

because we're already related
knowing that there's nothing we need to do
except allow ourselves to be.

Let's meet purely in presence
without any conditions or concepts
knowing that in essence we are the same
and that in being we are one.

The Clear Light of the Present

There is nothing that can't be undone —
no past injury that can't be healed
no past mistake that can't be corrected —
in the clear light of the present.

Every past action that arose from spite
can be redeemed by kindness
in the clear light of the present.

Every action that arose from ignorance
can be redeemed by wisdom
in the clear light of the present.

Painful memories of suffering
will evaporate like patches of fallen rain
in the clear light of the present.

And dark deep imprints of trauma
will uncover themselves so that they can be healed
in the clear light of the present.

Conflicts that have exhausted us
and grudges that have poisoned us
for lifetime after lifetime
can be flushed away in an instant

of pure compassion and forgiveness
in the clear light of the present.

There is no need for the past to shadow us
when we always live, and are always free
in the clear light of the present.

The Alchemy of Acceptance 1

Emptiness can be a vacuum
cold and hostile, dark with danger
or emptiness can be radiant space
glowing with soft stillness
and the only difference between them is acceptance.

A task may seem tedious
a chore to rush through reluctantly
or a task may seem rewarding
a process to relish, with an attentive mind
that reveals more richness, the more present you become
and the only difference between them is acceptance.

Pain may seem unbearable
searing through you from a sharp, concentrated point
so that you have no choice but to resist
to try to escape, to push away the pain
or pain can be a sensation
that you can move toward and merge with
that no longer has a center and dissipates through
    your being
until it becomes soft and numb, no longer pain at all
and the only difference between them is acceptance.

Trauma can break you down to nothing
destroy the identity you spent your whole life
    building up

like an earthquake that leaves you in ruins
or trauma can transform you
break open new depths and heights of you
give rise to a greater structure, a miraculous new self
and the only difference between them is acceptance.

Life can be frustrating and full of obstacles
with desires for a different life constantly disturbing
 your mind
or life can be fulfilling, full of opportunities
with a constant flow of gratitude for the gifts you have
and the only difference between them is acceptance.

Be Soft

for Russel Williams

Be soft
so that your mind doesn't clash with reality
and you can absorb your experience with ease.

Be soft
so that disappointments and insults don't bruise you
but bounce harmlessly away
after your softness has absorbed their force.

Be soft
so that thoughts don't turn to fixed ideas
and emotions flow through you without attaching
themselves
and animosity doesn't linger long enough to form a
grudge
and pain passes away before turning to trauma.

Be soft
so that you can bend with the wind without breaking
and become moist with the rain without flooding.

Be soft
so that you pass through the world without leaving
damage
only the lightest of trails that will dissolve like a cloud
and become part of the air that everyone breathes.

At One with Your Body

Lie down in silence.
Uncenter yourself from your restless mind.
Let your attention spread slowly through your body.
Feel your skeleton and skin, until you are one with them.
Feel the gentle breathing of your lungs
and the beating of your heart
and the flowing of your blood
until your attention merges with them.

Rest inside your body.
Let your limbs lie loose without pressure to move.
Let your face lie expressionless, without agitation.
Let your eyes and ears be dormant
without reaching out to perceive the world.

And when you are at one with your body
you can also be at one with your mind.

As your breathing slows down, your thoughts will
 slow down too.
As your body lies still, your mind will become still
 as well.

(After all, mind and body aren't separate entities.
They're telepathically attuned, like twins
who feel each other's pain and joy.)

And when your whole being is at rest
you'll sense a subtle spiritual essence
glowing softly like evening sunlight
through every atom of your limbs and veins and skin
and through the endless radiant space of your
    consciousness
from a source beyond both body and mind.

The Guru

I love to sit with my guru
so that I can absorb his radiance.

I love to ask him questions
so that, as he answers, he looks directly at me.
Then the whole room shimmers with golden light.
My mind slows down, and my being opens up
and my life energy flows softly through my body.
My solid skin and bone turn to vapor
until there is no outside or inside
and my ego self disappears like a ghost.

But I have another, even greater guru: the world.
I love to watch the clouds glide across the sky
flowing and foaming so gracefully.
I love to walk among the trees
and feel their calm wise sentience.
I love to gaze across the hills and fields
and sense the landscape's ancient soul.

As I watch, I'm filled with reverence.
My being falls still and silent, like a dumbstruck lover.
Waves of ecstasy flow through my body
revelations pour into my mind
and I'm lifted high above myself

emptied out and purified
by the beautiful is-ness of the world.

The space of the sky is my own space.
The soul of the landscape is my own soul.
And my guru is ever present and everywhere.

Making the Human Race Whole

Make as many connections as you can
so that this broken world can become whole again.

It's your responsibility
to radiate benevolence to everyone you meet
to be reckless with your friendliness
and to surprise strangers with your openness
on behalf of the whole human race.

It's your responsibility
to turn suspicion to trust, hostility to sympathy
to expose the absurdity of prejudice
to return hatred with implacable goodwill
until your enemies have no choice but to love you
on behalf of the whole human race.

It's your responsibility
to free yourself from bitterness
and to harness the healing power of forgiveness
to repair connections and reestablish bonds
that were broken by resentment years ago
on behalf of the whole human race.

It's your responsibility
to open up channels of empathy
through which compassion can flow

until there are so many connections
across so many different networks
that finally, like the cells of a body
billions of human beings will fuse together
sensing their common source
and their common core.

Then a new identity will emerge, an overriding
oneness.
And the human race will be whole, at last.

The Neutral Landscape

There's a moment before thought
when our life situation is neutral, neither good nor bad
like a landscape at the first light of dawn
that rests in quiet is-ness
without anyone to perceive it.

Then the mind wakes up
remembers its place in time and space
and surveys the situations that lie ahead
through filters of thoughts and fears.

Like a health and safety inspector
it imagines disastrous scenarios
and looks out for potential hazards.
And the landscape turns into a danger zone
full of predators and parasites
precarious paths and precipitous drops
and a thousand other things to dread.

But all the time, beneath the mind's projections
life remains just as it is —
a bright panorama of experience
that holds no problems, only situations
that we can always trust ourselves to deal with
if we approach them carefully
and give them our full attention.

I Accept You as You Are

There's no need to justify yourself
to apologize for your losses and failures
and the opportunities you've missed.
I don't see you as a failure or a loser.
I accept you as you are.

There's no need to tell me your life story
to share your past misfortunes
and your plans to reinvent yourself.
You're here with me now, without a future or a past
and I accept you as you are.

There's no need to pretend to be someone else
to impress me with your charm and intelligence
and keep talking to hold my attention.
I know the real you, beneath your surface self
and I accept you as you are.

You don't need to prove that you're worthy of my
affection.
I won't judge you because I understand you.
I won't reject you because I'm connected to you.
I can't hate you because I am you
and I love you as you are.

The House of Your Being

How can you live inside yourself
when the house of your being is full of discord
as if your siblings can't stop fighting
and your parents can't stop arguing
and the neighbors make too much noise
and the rooms are dirty and cluttered?

It's even worse when the house is empty
when the air is charged with anxiety
and the quietness seems alive with danger
so you can't relax for a moment.

It's no wonder you need to escape
and spend so much of your time outdoors
wandering the streets to pass the time
and only coming home to sleep.

But you can't escape from yourself forever.
No matter how far you run
you always have to come back home.
There's no point trying to live your life elsewhere
when you can never be anywhere but here.

So resist the pull that draws you outside.
Step inside yourself
and explore the house of your being.

Step slowly and lightly
from room to room and floor to floor
until the house becomes familiar again
and your presence pervades every space.

Soon the energy of your attention
will recharge the air with freshness.
Soon you'll sense a harmony
beneath the surface clutter.

And soon you won't feel uneasy when the house is
empty.
You'll relax and relish your inner peace.
At night the darkness will feel soft and rich, like velvet
and embrace you as you sleep.

And then you'll feel perfectly at home
within the house of your being.

Processes

The world isn't made up of objects
or discrete events that stop and start.
The world is made up of processes
that merge and feed and form one another
in an endless dynamic flow.

Listen — there are no isolated sounds
just flowing streams of noise
that arise and pass through your awareness.

Look — there are no individual sights or scenes
just the movement of forms through space
passing through your vision.

Time isn't made up of discrete moments
that pass out of the present and into the past.
Time is an endless flow of experience
that never stops being now.

The human race isn't made up of individuals
who live and die in separateness.
We're expressions of the same essence
like waves on the surface of the ocean.

We rise, take form, and fade and fall
as we pass through the process of life
then pass away and reemerge
as part of another process.

Empathy

Without empathy we see enemies everywhere.
We feel threatened by strangers when they come
close.
We strengthen our defenses and protect our resources
in case others try to steal what's rightfully ours.

But with empathy we see brothers and sisters.
When strangers come close we sense kinship.
We embrace them and open up our lives to them
knowing they're entitled to share what's ours.

Without empathy we feel incomplete.
The goal of our life is to accumulate —
to build an empire, to claim ownership of the world
so that one day we might feel whole.

But with empathy we feel no sense of lack.
The goal of our life is to contribute —
to alleviate suffering, to help heal the world
and strengthen our connection to the whole.

Without empathy the world seems full of
separateness.
The closer we look, the more separateness we see
and the essence of reality appears to be
tiny, solid building blocks of matter.

But with empathy the world is a unity.
The closer we look, the more connection we see
and the essence of reality reveals itself
as a vast space of formless oneness.

Without empathy other human beings are objects —
machines made up of inert materials
that we can use for our own ends
and discard once they have no more use.

But with empathy every person is a universe —
a mysterious spiritual space
full of unknown forces and energies
that we feel privileged to explore.

Without empathy the ego has a solid boundary.
We live as prisoners, trapped inside ourselves.
And the torment of our isolation
is redirected at the world as hatred.

But with empathy the self is soft and fluid.
We're part of the world, as the world is part of us.
And through our openness, like a river through a
 channel
we feel an endless flow of love.

If You Hurt Me

If you hurt me accidentally, I won't blame you.
If you bump into me on the street
tread on my toes, or trip me up, I won't mind at all.
I won't even be angry if you crash into my car
and I end up with serious injuries.
I might be upset or frustrated
but only with the random cruelty of life, not you.

How can I hate you for an accident?
Why should I feel any desire for revenge
when you have no bad intentions?

That would be like hating the rain
or cursing the sea for its coldness
and lashing out at its waves as they pass.

If it's not your fault, I'll forgive you
and accept your apologies readily.
If you're amenable, I might even hug you.

I might even be glad that you've hurt me
because it's brought out your natural kindness
and created a bond between us.

But what if you hurt me intentionally?
What if you plot and plan against me

spreading rumors, hurling insults
with a heart full of jealousy and hatred?
What if you rob me on the street
or attack me randomly or burgle my house?

Even then, I won't take it personally
and respond with cold malevolence.

I know that hatred isn't deep-rooted but caused by
 conditions
by feelings of fear or impotence
and a need for identity or certainty.

The source of hatred is unhappiness
and I feel sorry that you're unhappy.

So I will respond with respect
because I respect the part of you
that is deeper than thoughts and feelings.

So I will respond with love
because I love the part of you
that is purer than fear and hatred.

I love the unconditioned part of you
whose nature — like mine — is love.

When You Face Your Fears

When you avoid your fears, they grow and you
diminish.
Your soul contracts a little more
so that there's less space for light to reach you
and you become darker and colder inside.

But when you face your fears, you grow and they
diminish
and your soul opens up like a flower to the sun.

When you face your fears, you realize
that situations are never unbearable
if you're prepared to meet them fully.
There are secret reserves of resilience inside you
waiting for challenges to reveal themselves.

When you face your fears, you realize
that the ego is an unreliable narrator
who distorts the facts and exaggerates.
He always overstates danger
and always underestimates you.

When you face your fears, you realize
that the mind's projections and anticipations
cause much more suffering than reality itself.

When you face your fears, you realize
that you can never trust your thoughts.
But you can always trust your soul
to adapt and cope and overcome your fears.

Let Go of Your Pain

When your self-esteem has been wounded
by an insult or embarrassment
or when you've been mistreated or betrayed
and feel inflamed with a sense of injustice —
don't suppress your pain.
Allow yourself to feel hurt.

Let your pain express itself
then let it pass away.

Once you pick up pain, it attaches itself to you
and sticks to you ever more tightly
until you can't put it down again.

Don't keep replaying the incident
trying to make sense of it.
Like the sound from an old tape, its clarity will fade.
The details will grow vague
and you'll grow more confused.

And with each replay, the hurt will rise again
fermenting and growing more bitter
distilling more doubt and fear.

Hurt is a process that will play itself out
if you allow it to.

Don't ruminate anymore.
Leave your pain in the past
and bring yourself back to now.

And soon you'll sense your soul's resilience.
The most searing insults, the coldest rejections
even the cruelest of betrayals
will only hurt you temporarily.

Your soul has healing powers, like your body
and will make you whole again.

Creating Your Reality

If you look for reasons to be unhappy, you will
find them.
If you look for reasons to be contented, you will
find them.

If you want to worry, you will find problems.
If you want to appreciate your life, you will find
blessings.

If you want to criticize, you will find flaws.
If you want to love, you will find beauty.

You can survey your life situation
and select reasons to feel grateful
or reasons to complain.

You can anticipate the future
and select events to dread
or events to look forward to.

You can recollect the past
and select events that make you feel bitter
or events that make you feel proud.

And everything you select, positive or negative
is equally true and valid
or equally untrue and invalid.

So don't assume that your vision is clear and true.
When your mind makes judgments, be skeptical.

To the mind there are no truths, only possibilities
that become manifest when it selects them
like particles that are everywhere and nowhere
until an observer fixes them in one place.

But why create your own reality
when reality already exists?

Let the past sleep, let the future wait
and let the present exist as it is
without your interpretation.

Freedom from the Past

The past is always trying to pull us back
to the same old points of reference —
the mistakes and failures of our lives
when we took wrong turns
were overcome by obstacles
or let crucial opportunities pass by.

Our minds circle around those memories
like particles around a nucleus
spinning stories of alternate realities
parallel universes where we made the right choices
and our ambitions were fulfilled.

But the present is like a city
that can be reached from a thousand different roads.
Even if we had taken a different route
we would still be exactly where we are now.
The world would be exactly the same to us
and hold the same potential for happiness.

The present treats everyone equally
no matter where we've come from.

And the past can't enhance our happiness
except by fading away
and leaving us to now.

How Can I Express My Gratitude?

How can I express my gratitude
for this blissful beautiful morning
as I run down a muddy track toward the sea
with the blue sky expanding endlessly above me
and pure white sunshine pouring through space?

How can I express my gratitude
for my animal limbs that bend so lithely through the
 cool air
for my senses that open my awareness to this
 miraculous new day
as I find a tiny path between the rocks and climb
 down to the beach?

How can I express my gratitude
for the ocean that opens up in front of me
swelling and murmuring, like a lover who was always
 waiting
with a glorious trail of sunlight shimmering across
 her waves
and millions of incandescent sparks
dancing and flickering and flashing?

How can I express my gratitude
for this perfect eternal moment

as I undress and stumble over seaweed-covered
  stones toward the tide
then feel an electric shock of cold
as the ocean immerses and absorbs me?

The only way to express my gratitude
is to live ecstatically, without pettiness or fear
and to keep myself fluid and open and innocent
so that I am as radiant as the world
and worthy of the gift of life.

It's Hard to Be a Human Being

It's hard to be a human being
when you seem to be trapped inside yourself
with the rest of the world out there on the other side
and you feel insignificant and fragile, like a tiny island
surrounded by a vast roaring ocean
that's threatening to submerge you.

It's hard to be a human being
when you're forced to share your inner world
with a crazy whirling thought machine
that never stops churning and chattering
and makes you fear things that can't hurt you
and desire things that can't make you happy.

It's hard to be a human being
when you're so permeable to trauma
that ingrains itself deep inside you
and seems impossible to erase
and it's so easy to pick up attachments and habits
that grow stronger each time you express them
until they take over your life.

It's hard to be a human being
when the world is so chaotic and confusing

that you can't sense your right direction
or find a life that aligns with your purpose
so you feel inauthentic and unfulfilled
like an actor who hates the role she plays.

It's no wonder we feel restless and uneasy
as if this world isn't meant to be our home.
It's no wonder life seems a burden
and we spend so much time trying to escape from
ourselves.
It's no wonder we cause so much conflict
and leave trails of trauma everywhere we go.

But every strand of human hardship
can be traced back to the same source.

Our sufferings are the pains of separation.
We're lonely fragile fragments
who once felt part of the whole
and long for unity again.

Slow your life down
until you regain your sense of balance.
Let your mind fall silent
until you feel yourself reconnecting to the world.

And soon you will feel
the lightness of life living through you.

Soon you will sense
the harmony of belonging to the whole.

And then you will remember
how easy human life was meant to be.

Be Gentle with Your Mind

Be gentle with your mind.
Don't overload it with demands
or fill it with too much information
or pressurize it with too many deadlines
until it frazzles with strain
and can't function anymore.

Your mind isn't a machine; it's a sensitive artist.
It gets agitated easily if conditions aren't right.
Then inspiration fades and it can't give rise
to new ideas and insights.

Your mind is full of flowing energy, like a river
but it gets polluted easily, if you don't protect it
from stress and overstimulation.
Then the energy turns toxic
and makes you feel sick inside.

So be gentle with your mind.
Allow it to be filled with space
not clogged up with information.
Allow it to be soothed with stillness
not bombarded with stimuli.

And then your mind will serve you
with quiet and easy grace
and bring you an endless flow of gifts
from a place beyond the mind.

The Small Things

These days it's the small things that catch my
attention.
I'll always feel awestruck by sunsets, storm clouds,
and rolling hills
but I don't need to go out of my way to find beauty.
I see more than enough inside my house.

This morning I watched a wooden spoon floating in
the sink
motionless, facedown, with groups of soapsuds
circling slowly around it
like cells in some amniotic fluid.
Then I steamed some milk for my coffee
and watched enthralled as tiny bubbles flickered and
popped
inside a snowy mountain of froth.

I sat down to drink my coffee
and noticed a strange projection on the wall above —
a hazy shape of sunlight filled with swirling faint gray
lines
that danced and wove into one another
throwing off quick flashes
then slowing down and becoming still.

(It was only later that I realized
it was sunlight reflecting off the water in the sink
and shining onto the wall.)

My kitchen is filled with miracles.
The sacred and profane are one.
Each moment, no matter how seemingly mundane
contains the same sublime beauty as mountains and
skies
if you look closely enough.

The Landscape and the City (The Spirit and the Ego)

There was once a vast open landscape
where the air glowed softly with spirit
where the soil was rich with soul force
and the fields and forests were full of deep-green
    radiance.
The space that filled the landscape flowed into the sky
    above it
and into the universe beyond the sky.

But after centuries of stasis and harmony
the landscape was overrun with invaders
who cut down the trees and paved over the fields
and built houses and roads and bridges and walls.
A village became a town and then a city
that sprawled across the countryside.

And soon the inhabitants of the city
began to forget the world beyond it.
The city air was so hazy and the buildings so high
that people forgot there was a clear sky above them.
The city lights were so bright at night
that people forgot there was darkness around them.
And the city streets stretched so far and wide
that they forgot there was soil beneath them.

In the cramped gray space of the city
people lost touch with the spirit of the landscape.
They couldn't sense the radiance of the trees and
    fields
or the soul force of the earth.

And soon they began to feel oppressed
by the crowded noisy streets.
Soon they began to feel suffocated
by the heavy humid atmosphere of the city.

And one day the air was so full of tension
that a giant storm erupted.
The city's foundations began to shake
and its flimsy walls began to crumble.
Its buildings collapsed as if made of sand.

And when the survivors emerged from the ruins
they were dazzled by the brightness of the sun.
They felt overwhelmed by the endless space around
    them.
But soon their eyes adjusted to the light
and their souls expanded into the space.

And once the debris was cleared
the survivors formed a new kind of settlement —
not a town or even a village
but a quiet subtle system

that emerged out of the landscape organically
and blended with it naturally
without boundaries or distinction.

And without separation there was no suffering.
Everyone could feel their oneness with the landscape
and the oneness of the landscape with the whole
universe.
People felt the freshness of spirit all around them
caressing them like a soft warm breeze
and felt the deep rich soil of spirit beneath them
rooting and nourishing their being.

The Spiritual Teacher

You can't find contentment in this world
declared the spiritual teacher, waving his finger and
shaking his head.
The body is plagued by pain and discomfort.
Our minds are full of delusion.
The world is full of chaos and cruelty.
There is nothing but imperfection.

To be born is a great misfortune, he continued sternly,
like a schoolteacher breaking bad news to his class.
Life is full of restless striving.
Happiness always fades away
and leaves a bitter taste behind.
The goal of your life should be
to free yourself of desire
so that when you die you won't have to return
to this world of suffering.

I left the spiritual teacher
and walked through the park on my way home.

Clouds were rippling across the evening sky
as the sun flushed the horizon
with flames of incandescent orange.
Lines of trees were swaying with perfect grace.
The fields were luminous with emerald-green.

I felt the cool air brushing smoothly against my face
and heard the laughter of children on the
playground.

And I knew that the world is a miracle
and that life is a gift and a privilege
and that the teacher was mistaken.

The Role

It's not enough to be alive, they told you,
and it's not enough to be yourself.
While you're here on the surface of the earth
you have to take on a role.

They encouraged you to choose a role
that suited you and that you could carry off well.
But you didn't know how crucial your choice was.
Nobody told you that you might have to spend
your whole life playing the role.

At first the role was exciting.
Your soul felt raw and fragile
after years of childhood pain.
You weren't sure of your true identity
or if you could love or accept yourself.
So the role made you feel like you were someone
gave you strength and confidence
and separated you from your inner pain.

And soon you grew into the role.
You spent so much time in character
and learned to be so natural
that no one could tell you were acting, even you.

And as you became more proficient and confident
you lost touch with your true self.
Your persona took over
and convinced you it was the real you.

And now, after years of playing your role
you should feel proud of your achievements.
You should be savoring the success
that the role has brought you.

But instead you feel arid and empty.
There's a deep aching sadness inside you
and a desperate yearning for change
as if your soul is suffocating in darkness
and crying out for light and air.

And from the same dark depths of your being
you can feel the pain of the childhood wounds
that were buried alongside your true self
and have festered and become more toxic
through years of being left untreated.

So now you're clinging more tightly to your role
afraid of the pain that you've never faced
and afraid of letting go of your identity
because you're no longer sure what lies beneath.

But you know you have no choice.
There's only one way to avoid a living death.
There's only one way to heal your childhood pain.

It's time to let go of your role.

At first you'll feel confused.
There'll be a strange spaciousness and formlessness
like the empty space where a familiar building used
to stand.
Your life might seem purposeless
as if the path you were walking has disappeared
overnight
and there's no direction anymore.
And the trauma buried deep inside
may erupt and overwhelm you
like a dark wild river flooding your being.

But hold fast — you're stronger than you think.
The pressure of the pain will fade away
if you accept and observe and explore it.

And soon the healing will begin.
Your true self won't reject you but welcome you —
tentatively at first, with moments of unease
like a child who's reunited with a long-lost parent.

The healing will take time.
But you'll adjust to each other's presence
and gain each other's trust.

And as your true self grows more confident
and fills the space left by your role
your frustration and friction will dissolve.
You'll feel a new sense of wholeness and harmony.
And the world will seem strange and beautiful
as if you've been born again.

Now your life will flow organically
from your new authentic self.
Now you will live as you were meant to live
and become who you always were.

The Container

When bliss rises up inside you
it must have a strong container.
You have to be made of the finest clay
and be sturdy and well molded.
Make sure there are no cracks inside you
and that any past damage has been repaired.
Otherwise your bliss may break you.

When bliss rises up inside you
it must have a pure container.
Make sure that your surfaces are smooth
that old stains have been washed away
and there are no residues left inside
from the dark, acrid liquids you used to carry.
Otherwise your bliss may poison you.

Bliss can be volatile.
It needs the right conditions to settle
otherwise it becomes too dynamic
and vibrates too intensely and swells and spills.
Then you swing wildly from joy to despair
and can't focus or function in the world.

Bliss can be potent.
It needs the right conditions to mature.
Otherwise tiny spores of discord

germinate and multiply
and your bliss becomes corrupted
by the darkness that used to fill you.

So before you cultivate your bliss
and as you cultivate it
take care of your container.
Keep honing, cleansing, and strengthening it.

And then finally you will become
a perfect host
for a perfect joy.

Being a Body

It's hard to be a body
that seems to be decaying slowly
whose skin is slowly wrinkling and drying
whose energies take longer to replenish
and whose injuries take longer to heal.

It's hard to be a body
as it becomes more demanding and less obedient
like a child growing in reverse
in a process that can't be halted
where the pieces that assembled and arranged
themselves
so perfectly to create your form
will eventually disassemble and dissolve away
and release you back into emptiness.

It's hard to be a body
until you realize that the deepest impression you
make
is not through your appearance
but through the wholeness of your being
and the purity of your actions.

It's hard to be a body
until you stop trying to hold back time

and learn to flow with the slow transformation
of your form as you pass through this world.

It's easy to be a body
when you realize that the body is only partly you
and that the essence of you is an energy
that has no form and knows no time
and shines with ageless radiance
and can never decay or die.

Beyond Fear

Fear can't exist without fearful thoughts.
But one fearful thought can be incendiary
like an atom that starts a chain reaction.

An anticipation of danger, a memory of failure —
and that one thought spawns a host of others
that each spawn hosts of others
until your mental space is filled with turbulence
a swirling chaos of images and anticipations.

The thoughts grow denser, like gases solidifying
until you feel them as emotions
as panic that surges through your body
and anxiety that shivers through your veins.

So breathe deeply and slowly
until you sense some space inside you.
Feel the energy of being
flowing quietly through your body.

Then find a stable place, a vantage point
where you can stand still and watch the thoughts
    pass by
without being carried away.

And soon the space inside you will expand.
Soon a sense of calm wholeness will fill you.

Center yourself there —
open yourself to that spacious fullness.
And slowly the turbulence will fade away.
Soon your mind will be empty
like a clear sky after a storm has passed.

And then there will be no more fear.

Illness and Resurrection

Illness is inevitable
when we're weighed down by demands
and overwhelmed by information
and we've pushed ourselves so hard
that we've lost touch with our essence.

The pressure's too great and our being collapses.
It rebels and shouts, "Enough!"
and refuses to carry on.

At first you feel frustrated.
How can you be ill when there's still so much to do
when you've built up so much momentum
and covered so much ground?
Surely you'll fall behind now that you can't keep up?

But don't resist — it's time to rest.
Let solitude and quietness embrace you
until you feel rich, new energy seeping through
from the deep ground of your being
and beginning to replenish you.

The fragments of your being
will draw together and reassemble.
Your mind will slow down and settle again
like a lake after a storm, as silt sinks to the bottom.

And soon you'll reemerge
reattuned to your essence
realigned with your purpose
and ready to begin your life anew.

Your Spontaneous Self

Why look ahead and worry
that you won't be able to cope
with the challenges life offers you?

You should have learned by now
that there's a spontaneous self inside you
that's as agile as a wild animal
always ready to leap up
and respond with perfect reflexes
to any new situation.

You've only come this far
because your spontaneous self has been guiding you
steering you away from danger
(so gently that you weren't even aware of the danger)
whispering wisdom into your ears
and arranging crazy coincidences
(so carefully that you thought they were just random).

Your spontaneous self will never let you down
as long as you don't obstruct it
as long as your mind isn't so dense with doubt and
    fear
that impulses can't flow through you.

Life is a game that moves much faster than thought.
Your sluggish mind is bound to fall behind.

But you can trust your spontaneous self
to meet every moving moment
with a perfect instinctive response.

We Can Only Be Sure of the Present

We can never be sure of the future.
So many different processes are flowing
that we can't predict how they'll coalesce
or what events they'll produce.

We can never be sure of the past.
Our memories have been filtered through
so many foggy layers of thought
that they aren't a reliable record.

We can only be sure of the present
where reality streams straight through our senses
and we know the world directly and immediately
through the clear light of experience.

All of This Is inside You

Don't believe that your life is worthless
and that it doesn't matter if you waste it.
Don't believe that your life is arbitrary
and that it doesn't matter what you do.
Don't believe that your life is meaningless
and that the universe wouldn't miss you if you
 disappeared.

How can you be worthless when you are the cosmos?
How can your life be purposeless
when you're the miraculous manifestation
of billions of years of unfolding?

From the beginning of time to now
elements have been coalescing, creating higher forms
becoming ever more complex and intricate
and ever more spacious and sentient
leading all the way to you.

Your being is an ancient torch.
At first it was a tiny flame that sparked out of silent
 blackness
and flickered unsteadily for millions of years.
Countless other unknown forms carried it and
 nurtured it
and the flame grew brighter and stronger

until it was passed on to you
as an incandescent, white-hot glow.

Your purpose is the purpose of the universe.
Your meaning is the meaning of the universe.

All of this is inside you.
All of this informs you.
Your life is all of this.

Rising Above

There's so much messiness to rise above —
the discord of relationships
the pettiness of resentment and jealousy
and the frustrations of illness and tiredness.

There's so much triviality to rise above —
the drudgery of chores and draining demands
the endless juggling of arrangements and deadlines
the constant nagging needs of the body and mind.

There's so much meanness to rise above —
the inner lack that makes us hunger
for power and possessions
and the ego separateness that makes us numb
to the sufferings of others.

That's why we have to find a purpose
that lifts us above the messiness.
That's why we have to find a meaning
that immunizes us to the pettiness.

That's why we have to reach
a place of pure and timeless truth
where wisdom is waiting
to be expressed and embodied
and transmitted to future generations.

Every act of selflessness
is a triumph of unity over separateness.
Every artistic creation
is a triumph of truth over triviality.

And then, once we've risen above
we have to come back down again
to share our truth and insight.
We have to illuminate the world below
with the light we've gathered from above.

Then the world will be transfigured.
The mundane will be touched with the miraculous
and discord will be filled with harmony.

Something Better

"There must be something better,"
says a voice inside your head —
a better place than where you are now
a quicker route than the one you're taking
a more suitable role than the one you're playing
a more fulfilling life than the one you're leading.

But no matter how you rearrange your life
something never seems quite right.
Every time you change your place
happiness still eludes you
and you wonder if you should ever have left
the place you started from.

So don't succumb to the allure of the other.
Tell yourself that this is the place
you're meant to be, at least for now.
Let your present situation be
your entire world, at least for now.

Then you'll sense something far better
than the discord of endless desires:
the ease and grace of acceptance
and the joy of truly being where you are.

I Love the Days

I love the days of doing nothing
when time stops hovering over my shoulder
pointing and shouting directions.

I love the days with no direction
when we ignore itineraries and turn off road
and wander through wild open spaces
without moving forward or backward.

I love the days of no expectations
of not deciding anything in advance
or not deciding anything at all
depending on the needs
of each unfolding moment.

I love the days of not needing
to be anywhere but now.

I love the days of not being productive
that become the most productive of all.

I love the days of doing nothing
that become gloriously full of being.

When the Mind Is Quiet

We're always alone with our thoughts —
always looking out from a place inside ourselves
at a world that's on the other side.
And the otherness of the world seems unsettling
like a different country full of strange landscapes and
customs
where we can never feel fully at home.

And as our thoughts grow busier, the boundary
strengthens.
The world recedes and becomes more unreal —
colors fade away, sounds become muffled
as if a window pane is thickening, becoming mistier,
making us feel more abstracted and isolated.

And in the end we can barely tell the difference
between the hazy shapes outside our window
and the shadowy thoughts inside.

But when our minds are quiet we're never alone.
A quiet mind makes connections.
Walls and windows dissolve away —
our being flows out into the world
and the world flows into us.

When your mind is empty
the whole world can fill you.

When your mind is quiet
you're never alone
but always at one.

Your Body

Your body doesn't want you to detach yourself from it
to lose yourself in abstraction and forget it's there.

It doesn't want you to see it as a beast
whose instincts debase you, whose functions demean
you
and whose desires corrupt your purity.

It doesn't want you to see it as a burden
whose ailments disturb you
and whose demands irritate you.

It doesn't want you to see it as a cage
that imprisons you and that one day you'll escape
from
when death disconnects your mind and body
and you ascend into the ether, like a bird flying free.

Your body wants you to relax
to focus your attention outside yourself
until your thoughts slow down
and space opens up inside you
and your sense of self expands
beyond the cramped space of your mind
through your chest and arms and your waist and legs
through your bones and veins and muscles and organs

until every molecule of your being
is alive with your energy and attention.

Your body wants you to realize
that it's just as sacred as your soul
and that every intricate movement of your limbs
every hair, every wrinkle, every substance you secrete
and every microscopic miracle that takes place inside
you
from moment to moment to keep you healthy and
alive
is just as much an expression of spirit
as any profound thought or sublime state of being.

Your body wants you to realize
that you can't split yourself in two
because everything it does is you.

There is no higher or lower.
There is no sacred or profane.
There are just different aspects of spirit
equally perfect and pure.

Coming Down from the Mountain

It's easy to be a monk in the mountains
or a hermit in the desert
and see God in the silence and empty space.

It's easy to be still
when no winds are blowing around you.
It's easy to be enlightened
when your world never turns toward the dark.

But what happens when you come down from the
mountain
and noisy city streets disturb your serenity
and messy human relationships interfere
with your connection to the divine
and the demands of daily life pull you away
from your self-sufficient wholeness?

Away from the stillness of the mountain
the fragile flame of your enlightenment
will soon be extinguished
and the darkness that overwhelms you
will feel cold and deep and empty.

Stillness can only endure
when it has been built up
in the midst of turbulence.

Enlightenment can only endure
when it has grown deep and strong
in the midst of darkness.

Slow Down

The world keeps speeding up, moving much too fast.
That's why it's full of chaos
and why it's heading for catastrophe.

Slow down.
Don't be so desperate to reach the future
that you push the present away.

Treat each moment with respect
as a friend who deserves your attention.

Greet every new experience as a guest
who's welcome to be part of your life.

Slow down
and feel how the stress of doing
turns into ease of being.

Slow down
and feel how your rigid separateness
softens into spacious belonging.

Slow down
and see how the future fades like a mirage
and how the present arises around you
as clear and fresh as dawn.

We Are Each Other

We're not ghostly entities
marooned inside our mental space
with our personal pain and suffering
that can never be shared or understood.

We're not machines full of selfish genes
who are always scheming to outdo each other
and only ever show kindness
if there's some benefit to ourselves.

We are each other.
Every human being's feelings flow
like currents of air through the atmosphere
of our communal being —
brushing each other's souls
touching each other's hearts
stirring mutual compassion.

We feel compassion because we're connected.
We sense each other's suffering
because we share each other's being.
We risk our lives for others
because there is only one life.
We help and heal and love each other
because we are each other.

The Two Worlds

Every moment we have a choice
to be absent or to be present
to be elsewhere or to be here.

Elsewhere is the place where doubt and regret live —
a dull gray netherworld
full of the ghosts of past events
and shadows of the future.

Elsewhere is the place where fear thrives —
a plateau full of risks and threats
where we're always exposed, like animals
who are hunted by different predators.

Elsewhere is the place where desires grow —
a desert full of mirages
that tempt us with ambitions that can't fulfill us
and pleasures that can't satisfy us
and leave us gasping and panting
with a thirst that can't be quenched.

But here is a bright spring morning
where the whole world stands pristine and clear
and each moment is sufficient to itself
and there is nothing that lives or grows
apart from what is and was meant to be.

Here is a beautiful landscape
of translucent light and infinite space
and deep rich colors and perfect forms
and endless intricate details —
a masterpiece that is freshly painted every moment.

Here there is no lack
only the wholeness of what is now.
Here there is no doubt
only the certainty of now.
Here there is no complexity
only the simple truth of now.

So why choose absence when we can be present?
Why be elsewhere when we can be here?

If Time Disappeared for a Moment

If time disappeared for a moment
and the human race was free of the past
every other species would be startled
as a strange new silence fell upon the earth
and the madness that they are so accustomed to
subsided for a moment.

If time disappeared for a moment
and the human race was free of the past
we would let go of ancient grudges
and be unable to tell enemies and friends apart.
Soldiers would suddenly drop their weapons
wondering why they were fighting their brothers.
Zealots would stop ranting midsentence
wondering why they were telling so many lies.

If time disappeared for a moment
and the human race was free of the past
the labels that define and separate us
would crumble to pieces like paper masks.
Centuries of fixed ideas and false beliefs
would blow away like dead leaves from a tree
leaving us naked and no different from each other.

If time disappeared for a moment
and the human race was free of the past

we would offload our old resentments
and be cleansed of our toxic bitterness
and step free of the shadows of guilt
that have stalked us throughout our lives.

We would dance with lightness and glee
as if celebrating the coming of spring
and then look around and be amazed
at the pristine beauty of the world
that before we could see only
through a dense distorting prism.

For a moment our hearts will be pure
and for a moment we will be at peace.

You Are Not the Process

Sometimes it's demeaning to watch thoughts pass by
and realize how judgmental and petty they can be.
It's like being sober at a drunken party
cringing as friends make fools of themselves.

"Can this really be me?" you ask yourself, ashamed.
"Is my mind really so full of nonsense?"

But whoever said these thoughts were yours?
Thinking is a process that takes place inside you
like digestion or the circulation of your blood.
And you are not your thoughts
any more than you are your digestion.

Pay as little attention to your thoughts
as you do to your circulating blood.
Take the content of your thoughts as seriously
as the contents of your intestines.

And soon your thoughts will slow down and fade away
into a background noise that doesn't disturb you
like the hum of a small television set, turned down low
flickering in a corner of a room.

And then you'll look inside yourself
and find nothing to be ashamed of.

The Flow

Don't make a mental map of your journey
and imagine yourself moving forward
counting down your steps
and anticipating the joy of arrival.

Your anticipation will stretch time.
Your imagination will magnify distance.
You'll feel frustrated by your lack of progress
overwhelmed by the effort ahead of you
until you slow down and stop, defeated.

Don't push away moments as if they're obstacles.
Embrace the nowness of your journey.
Instead of staring tensely straight ahead
let your vision stretch easefully around you.

And soon, when your mind is empty of the future
and quietly full of the present
you'll latch on to the flow of the journey
and relax into its gentle rhythm.

And like a river the flow will carry you
all the way to your destination.

Back Home

Wherever I go in the world
I am always at home in the sea.

When strange cities seem overwhelming
and other cultures seem incomprehensible
and human beings seem suspicious
the ocean always welcomes me
with easygoing tenderness.

She senses my presence straight away
like an animal that remembers my scent.
And as soon as her cool tide touches my feet
I feel the ancient bond between us.
As I swim she massages my limbs
until I'm free of the tensions of land-based life.

No matter how much chaos human beings cause
as we scurry across islands and continents
the ocean is steadfast and nonchalant.
She knows she will outlive us all.

Every morning since the beginning of time
sparks of sunlight have danced across her waves
gleefully, just like this morning.
And every night since the beginning of time

white ribbons of moonlight have streamed across
her waves
majestically, just like last night.

Right at the beginning of time
the sound of her roaring rumbling rush began
and has never paused for a moment since
never even changed tone or pitch.

The ancient mother
who gave birth to life
hundreds of millions of years ago
and who embraces all her children
whenever they return.

The Longing

You feel restless and uneasy but don't know why.
No matter how many ambitions you fulfill
no matter how many desires you satisfy
your frustration never seems to fade away.
Contentment always seems to elude you.

But trace your desires back to their source.
No matter how they disguise themselves
they all stem from a sense of lack.

You don't feel frustrated because you haven't achieved
enough
or because you're being deprived of what's rightfully
yours
or because you're being plagued by misfortune
but because you were never meant to be separate.

Beneath your lust for power, possessions, and
pleasures
you ache to be one with the world.

And there's no need to be timid or to suppress your
desire
because the world wants to be one with you.
She feels your absence, senses your unease
and she's pulling you toward her

with a soft magnetic radiance
that shimmers through the space between you.
She's sending subtle signals, chemical messages
 that say:
We belong to each other.

And now that you know the true nature of your
 desire
and that your love is reciprocated
there'll be no more delay or diversion.

Soon the universe will celebrate
your ecstatic marriage —
a timeless consummation
in which separateness dissolves
and frustration fades away
and your longing is fulfilled.

The Forest

All your life you've been told that the forest is
dangerous
so thick that sunlight never touches its soil
so wild that no one finds their way back out
once they've wandered inside.

You've heard stories of wolves and bears
prowling hungrily through the forest
and tales of ghostly shapes and shades
that fill the air at night.

So you've spent your life outside the forest
skirting its edges and watching your steps
looking away and trying to forget
that you're always in its shadow.

Once when you were brave and curious
you couldn't resist glancing inside.
And ever since you've been haunted by what you saw:
a melee of shifting sounds and shapes
a menacing darkness, full of strange forces and
energies.

And still now, although you try to close your ears
at night you can hear the murmurings
of sinister forest creatures.

But listen more closely:
those aren't the whispers of ghosts or the howls of
animals.
It's the voice of your deepest self
calling you back home
telling you that it's time to turn inside.

So step into the forest.

At first you might be startled
by the unfamiliar noises
and the wrinkled twisted barks and stretching
branches.
But don't turn back — be courageous.
The discord is only superficial.

A few steps farther, and a hush descends.
The fresh stillness of the forest engulfs and enters you
spreading slowly through your being like mist.

And the farther you go the more stillness you sense —
an atmosphere of ease, an energetic calmness
a sentience that's both soothing and enlivening.

And finally you find yourself
at the heart of the forest
where a glade opens out between the trees —
a deep wide space full of lush green grass
luminous with sunlight from a clear still sky.

You can lie down and rest here, free from fear
at the radiant source of your being.

And then you'll wonder why
you were ever afraid of yourself.

The Strangeness

I've lived in my house for fifteen years —
I've walked the same streets every day
seen the same buildings, the same trees, and the same
    sky —
but I still sense strangeness around me.

This morning, like so many other mornings
I cross the road on my way to the shops.
And I'm struck by the perfect geometry of the houses
with their sloping roofs and rectangular walls
and jigsaw patterns of bricks.

I'm struck by patterns of shadows on the pavement
thrown by railings and gates and fences.
I'm struck by the reflections flashing
from the windows of parked cars.
I'm struck by the waves and spirals of cloud above me
in forms that have never been seen before
and will never be seen again.

Why should the familiar become mundane?
As long as my senses are keen
and as long as my mind is quiet
the world will always be strange.

Each moment arises as a newborn world
without reference to the past.

Loss

In every loss there is liberation.

When we're adrift in the future
chasing after goals and ambitions
loss pulls us back to the present.

When illusions of success and status
have inflated our self-importance
loss returns us to reality
and reminds us of our insignificance.

When our minds are full of confused desires
loss disentangles us
and simplifies our lives
so that we have space to grow.

When layers of dull contentment
are suffocating our souls
loss strips us naked
so that the world can touch us freshly
and we can feel alive again.

When there are too many attachments inside us
obscuring our true nature
loss empties out our being
and reconnects us to our essence.

Loss breaks down our identity
so that our broken fragments
can fuse together again
at a higher level of order.

In loss we find ourselves again.

Your Endeavors

If the aim of your endeavors
is to increase your own status and success
then your achievements will always be
as narrow as yourself.

Your ambitions and attachments
will block your creativity.
Self-centered thoughts will fill your mind
leaving no space for ideas to form.

And as you ponder over your actions
doubts will dampen your confidence
fears will drain your courage
until your sense of purpose fades away
like a stream that dries up on arid land.

But if the aim of your endeavors
is to help and serve and contribute
then your achievements will be as wide as the world.

A higher purpose will flow through you like a river
from a mysterious sacred source.
New insights and ideas will keep rising
from the fertile open space of your mind.

Doubts and fears will evaporate
through the energy of your inspiration
and the power of your purpose.

Then there will be no limit to your achievements
and no limit to your joy.

Perfection

Don't be ashamed of your weakness.
Nobody ever expected you to be completely pure.
Nobody ever expected you to be completely free
of pride and greed and lust.

You're not a monk or hermit
who keeps himself pure by hiding from the world.
You're not a disembodied spirit
who has no instincts to satisfy
and no desires to control.

Down here life is a teeming marketplace
full of stress and stimulation.
It's not easy to stay stable
when the crowd keep pushing and pulling you.
It's not easy to abstain
when the traders keep offering you their goods.

Accept your impurity
even as you try to purify yourself.
Accept that you will never be completely pure
and that there is no need to be.

You are already perfect
in your imperfection.

For a Moment

for Mary Oliver

Forget the demands of your day for a moment.
Ignore the bullying thoughts
that remind you of what needs to be done.
Step aside and let the world rush forward
without you for a moment.

Why give yourself to the future?
Give yourself to the nowness
of sunshine and reflections and shadows
and the humming of household appliances
and the smooth animal motions of your body
as you walk or eat or wash.

Why give yourself to busyness?
Give yourself to the stillness
of furniture and plants and ornaments
and of the space that fills your room.

There is no urgency.
Nothing will be lost
if the world has to wait
a little longer for your contributions.

There is nothing that needs your attention
as much as the nowness of the world.

There is nothing that you need to do
as much as you need to be.

The Search

When did you lose yourself?
You can't remember — it was so long ago.
But ever since then you've been searching
scanning every obscure forgotten place
lifting up every unlikely object
and feeling more frustrated every day.

And now you're starting to forget
exactly what you're looking for
like a dazed and weary soldier
who can't remember why he's fighting.

Soon you'll lose heart and abandon the search.
But you won't feel disappointed —
you'll feel relieved, as if a burden has been lifted
and you're free to start living again.

And one day when you feel attuned to yourself again
free of the stress and strain of the search
you finally find what you're looking for
in the closest, most obvious place:
the essence of your being, shining clearly
like a beautiful luminous jewel.

Why did it wait so long to reveal itself?

You were looking too hard to see something so subtle
searching in one place for something that's
everywhere
hoping for a miracle that only happens
when you give up hoping
looking for a truth that you can only find
when you give up looking.

But you weren't just seeking, you were preparing —
purifying and emptying and opening yourself
until finally you were ready
to see what was always there
and find what you always had.

An accidental discovery
that your whole life has prepared you for.

Moments of Happiness and Sadness

In moments of great happiness
remember that happiness is a state of mind
created by patterns of events
that are constantly in motion
like weather conditions that sometimes produce
beautiful bright warm days.

So be grateful for your happiness, and relish it
knowing that it will fade away.

In moments of deep sadness
remember that sadness is a state of mind
created by patterns of events
that are constantly in motion
like weather conditions that sometimes produce
miserable dull cold days.

So acknowledge your sadness, and accept it
knowing that it will fade away.

Every Morning When I Wake Up

Every morning when I wake up, I re-create myself.

I emerge from formless consciousness
like a diver rising to the surface, still immersed in
    bliss.
And slowly I remember the world and who I am.

The past pieces itself together like a jigsaw.
The future forms in front of me like a road.
I remember the roles I play, the concepts I've
    collected
the beliefs that define me, and the ambitions that
    remind me
of who I'm supposed to be becoming.

And soon the fragments have reassembled.
The building blocks are in place.
I'm ready to resume my life.

I accept my constructed self.
It plays a necessary role.
Why should I resent it
when there's no disparity between us?

All the time throughout the day
I sense my uncreated self
stretching deep beneath my surface
nourishing me with peace and joy
informing with me the formless.

If

If you can find out who you really are
beneath the habits and opinions you've absorbed
and the conventions you unthinkingly follow —

If you can distinguish the deep impulses of your soul
from the shallow desires of your ego
and let streams of thought pass through your mind
without latching on or listening —

If you can sense the sun of your true self
behind layers of cloudy concepts and constructs
and keep your mind open and clear
so that soul force shines through everything you do —

Then that's all you ever need to achieve.

There's no need to search for answers
if you're expressing the truth that's inside you.
There's no need to look for meaning
if you've found the path you were meant to follow.

It doesn't matter whether you're applauded or
ridiculed
whether you make a mark on the world
or live and die in obscurity.

If you can do what you're supposed to do
and be exactly who you're meant to be —

That's all you ever need to achieve.

The Reality of Connection

It's easy to hate in abstraction.
It's easy to make mental enemies
based on old stories of insults and intrigues
that you've been told by others
or new stories of hurt and resentment
that you create with your own thoughts.

It's much harder to hate in reality
in the presence of real human beings.

Sit opposite your enemy in a quiet room.
Look into her eyes in silence.

Anger and anxiety might sweep through you at first
but soon a connection will form.
Beneath the surface of your minds
a secret exchange of empathy will begin
a flow of fellow feeling between your souls.

Souls have no thoughts or memories
and so they feel no hatred.
Souls only feel their oneness, their common core.
In presence they draw together
like children who smile and start to play
while their parents are busy arguing.

And soon your perspective will begin to shift.
Resentment will slowly melt away.
Your enemy will become your equal, your fellow
human being
who deserves your respect and forgiveness.

Abstract hatred can't survive
when reality is connection
and reality is love.

Your Being Belongs to the Present

Your ego mind belongs to the past.
Like a museum, everything in it comes from the past —
beliefs that were handed down from your parents
ideas you absorbed from your culture
thought patterns that formed when you were young
old traces of trauma that still cause you pain
and random memories that keep replaying.

And your thoughts keep dragging you back to the past
like old friends who are jealous of your new life
and keep making you revisit
the haunts you've left behind
and the habits you've long outgrown.

But your being belongs to the present.
It has never known anything but the present.
It only knows the past and future as ideas
that pass through its nowness, like clouds through the
sky.

Untangle yourself from thoughts and concepts.
Give your full attention to your experience
until the structures of your mind grow soft
and you feel the calm wholeness of being
seeping through your inner space
and bringing you back to presence.

Slip outside your ego mind
and leave the past behind.

Then your life will be an adventure —
an exhilarating voyage of discovery
through the endless spacious freshness of presence.

The Gift

As you breathe, inhale deeply
in gratitude for the gift of air.

As you eat, swallow slowly
in gratitude for the gift of food.

As you see, look attentively
in gratitude for the wonder of the world.

As you love, be passionate
in gratitude for the beauty of flesh and form.

As you live, be authentic and fearless
in gratitude for the gift of life.

The Alchemy of Acceptance 2

Old age may be a process of decay
that withers your body and mind
and poisons you with bitterness
as you yearn for the freshness of youth.

Or old age may be a process of liberation
that enriches you with wisdom
and makes you more present as the future recedes
and lightens your soul as you let go of attachments.

And the only difference between them is acceptance.

Death may be a cold black emptiness
that mercilessly devours your ego
and makes everything you own seem valueless
and everything you've achieved seem meaningless.

Or death may be a perfect culmination
a soft twilight at the end of a long summer's day
when you're filled with heavy tiredness and ready to
    sleep
and know that you will wake up again to a bright new
    dawn.

And the only difference between them is acceptance.

The Wave

The ocean sighed with pleasure
as the wind caressed and stroked her
and soon the wave was born.

The wave felt his oneness with the ocean.
He felt her as his source, as part of his own being
and knew he could never exist apart from her.

But soon the wave began to watch himself.
He saw his own smooth and graceful motion
and was mesmerized.
He saw the beautiful bubbling foam that sprayed
    around him
and was transfixed.

The wave fell in love with himself.
He started to believe that he was his own master
that it was his own strength that was propelling him.
He believed that he was directing his own flow
and could change direction if he wanted.

The wave forgot the ocean, and saw himself as
    separate —
a self-sufficient, sea-less wave.
He felt proud of his power, exhilarated by his autonomy
as he rolled faster and rose higher.

But then he looked around and saw the other waves —
the ones who had already peaked and crashed
and were beginning to dip and to disperse
and the others who were already dissolving,
    disappearing.

The wave felt afraid, realizing that his form was
    temporary
that his speed and power would ebb away
and soon he would dissolve and disappear as well.

He felt alone as he sensed the empty space around
    him
and saw the distance between him and the other waves.
He felt threatened by the ocean's vastness
now that he seemed to be separate from it.

The wave resisted and rebelled.
He tried to build up more momentum, to collect
    more water
to roll more smoothly, to foam more spectacularly
to make himself so powerful that he would never
    dissolve away
to make his form so perfect that he could escape
    decay.

But soon he realized that he had no choice
that he had less control than he thought, less strength
    than he thought.

He knew he couldn't resist the flow of life
and hold back time and tide.

The wave stopped grasping and pushing
and felt the relief of letting go
and the freedom of no longer trying.

After his majestic foaming rush
and the glorious crescendo of his breaking
he gave himself up to his ebbing fading flow
and to the ease of his descent.
And he was filled with the joy of acceptance.

The wave allowed his boundaries to soften
and felt his connection to every other wave
and his oneness with the whole of the ocean.
He felt the vast wholeness of the ocean
within his own being
then as his own being.

And then the wave dipped, slowed down, and began
to dissipate.
Quietly and serenely, without fear or resistance
he gave himself to the tide
and became the ocean again
knowing that he had never been anything else.

Acknowledgments

I would like to express my gratitude to my poetic adviser Susan Miller for many helpful comments and suggestions. I originally posted many of these poems/reflections on my social media pages or in my monthly newsletter — thanks to everybody who responded with encouragement or feedback. I am also deeply grateful to the team at New World Library and to Eckhart Tolle and Kim Eng for their support over the past few years.

Index of First Lines

About the Author

Steve Taylor is the author of several bestselling books on spirituality and psychology, including *The Leap* and *Waking from Sleep*. He is the author of two previous poetic books, *The Meaning* and *The Calm Center*. He also writes a popular blog for *Psychology Today* called *Out of the Darkness*. He lives in Manchester, England.

www.stevenmtaylor.com

About Eckhart Tolle Editions

Eckhart Tolle Editions was launched in 2015 to publish life-changing works, both old and new, that have been personally selected by Eckhart Tolle. This imprint of New World Library presents books that can powerfully aid in transforming consciousness and awakening readers to a life of purpose and presence.

Learn more about Eckhart Tolle at

www.eckharttolle.com

NEW WORLD LIBRARY is dedicated to publishing books and other media that inspire and challenge us to improve the quality of our lives and the world.

We are a socially and environmentally aware company. We recognize that we have an ethical responsibility to our readers, our authors, our staff members, and our planet.

We serve our readers by creating the finest publications possible on personal growth, creativity, spirituality, wellness, and other areas of emerging importance. We serve our authors by working with them to produce and promote quality books that reach a wide audience. We serve New World Library employees with generous benefits, significant profit sharing, and constant encouragement to pursue their most expansive dreams.

Whenever possible, we print our books with soy-based ink on 100 percent postconsumer-waste recycled paper. We power our offices with solar energy and contribute to nonprofit organizations working to make the world a better place for us all.

Our products are available wherever books are sold. Visit our website to download our catalog, subscribe to our e-newsletter, read our blog, and link to authors' websites, videos, and podcasts.

customerservice@newworldlibrary.com
Phone: 415-884-2100 or 800-972-6657
Orders: Ext. 110 • Catalog requests: Ext. 110
Fax: 415-884-2199

www.newworldlibrary.com